The Secret of Abraham's children

One New People

Am Chadash Echad

You Have Been Handpicked by God...

Table of Contents

Prologue

The only people promised freedom from debt are Abraham's children

Find the Secret of Abraham's Children, and how to claim your inheritance

From ancient days, the Jewish Bible foretold that all Nations would be brought into Israel -

The Lord says –
It is too small a thing that You My servant will raise up the scattered tribes of Jacob only, and restore to Me the remnant of Israel. I have anointed You to be the Light to all Nations, to show My salvation to the ends of the earth, and bring My Covenant to every people, nation, and language under the sun.
Isaiah 49:6 (NJCV)

New Covenant Jewish prophets declared that the Jews and those from the Nations would become One New People in Yeshua (Jesus) the Messiah -

Yeshua (Jesus) the Messiah fulfilled the Law of Moses, completing all of its sacrifices and rules, choosing out of all Nations One New People set apart for Himself. He is the Way through Whom all who call upon Him become One in the Prince of Peace. Ephesians 2:15 (NJCV)

The Messiah gave Himself to redeem us. Now He says that we must love and serve Him above all things -

All who want to be my student and learn My ways, must cling to me more than to parents, wife, children, or earthly relatives - more than to

all of their own wishes and desires. You can't be my student without giving up everything else for me. To be able to learn My ways, you must hate everyone and everything else by comparison - even leave behind your own life. Luke 14 (NJCV)

We know that we can never be perfect, but we also know that He forgives us every single day by His grace.

A believer can make a lot of mistakes, and still make it to Heaven. But the more obedience, the greater the rewards - because these blessings come from a covenant relationship with God. You cannot go against the Covenant and expect blessings. You have to keep the Covenant to get the blessings. You who were from the Nations have now been made a light to all Nations. Fulfill your destiny and you will be blessed.

Abraham's Children

How the devil is blocking the blessings you inherited from the Jews

What this book is about -

You may find the pages in this book incredible, astonishing, maybe even shocking - but in this book you will also find Scripture to back up every statement.

As you know, Scripture is always true, and it always works when you believe it.

The main reason believers today often have little or no power, little or no victory over devils, not enough healing, not enough money - is simple - these blessings are all promised to the Jews.

Christians - followers of the Messiah - have had their eyes darkened to their true inheritance and actual identity.

In this book you will find out who you really are in Christ the Messiah - but we will use the Hebrew words that the Greek words were based on. Christ is Greek for "Mashiach" or "Messiah the Anointed One".

Yeshua (Jesus) was anointed with the Holy Spirit without measure. There is no limit to His power, wisdom, and kingdom.

A Christ-ian is actually a Messiah-ian. A follower, a student, of the Messiah - who is God Almighty.

Our Messiah (Savior) can speak today from Heaven - and change any circumstance in your life. Sometimes He changes it instantly, sometimes he changes it over time.

Our Messiah is the Son of Man - specifically the Son of David the Seed of Abraham.

That's where it gets really interesting -

All of us who are in Messiah Jesus - have become the Seed (Children) of Abraham.

Abraham was and is the friend of God - and in his children and descendants is all the blessing that is, or ever will be, on the earth.

One thing is for sure true - if you are a child of Abraham, you are blessed, and you will be blessed.

All the Jews (including the ones who have been scattered into the Nations) are children of Abraham. If they believe in the Messiah, they have the highest blessing a person can have on this earth. If they don't believe, they will go to hell even while having advantages during their lifetimes.

And here's the secret the devil doesn't want you to know - if you believe in the Messiah, you have become a true child of Abraham, and <u>you have inherited each and every blessing that any Jew will ever have</u> if they believe in the Messiah. Because you have actually become a Jew, spiritually, physically, and in every way.

When you read that last paragraph, I know that your spirit said "yes!" - but your mind said, "*what??*"

Your spirit has been made alive by Messiah, and knows all things - but your mind has to be renewed by the Word. And there's a few things your mind hasn't learned yet - because they have been hidden from you by the devil in an attempt to steal your inheritance and blessings.

You have inherited the blessings of the Jews.

That's a fact, as you'll soon see, it's written clearly in the Bible.

As your mind begins to understand and take hold of this truth, your life will begin to change.

Read this book again and again - get it into your

spirit. Tell your friends and family about it so they can be blessed too.

The Jews have been Jews for thousands of years, they've had lots of practice being Jews. You just got saved maybe a few years ago, and didn't know yet that you were a Jew, much less how to live like one.

You're about to find out, and start your journey to a supernatural life like you never thought possible before.

Foreword

What if you woke up one morning and God had decided to make you Jewish?

You now had amazing favor with God...

How would your life change?

**Are you one of
Abrahams Children**

Claim Your Inheritance Now
...before the devil steals it

Who are Abraham's children?
It's an important question because so many things depend on the answer.

Naturally you would expect the devil to try to confuse the issue
Because it is clear that Abrahams children are the ones who will be in heaven - and who will also be blessed while on earth -

But concerning the resurrection of the dead, have you not read what was spoken to you by God, who said: 'I am the God of Abraham, the God of Isaac, and the God of Jacob'? He is not the God of the dead but of the living.   Matthew 22.31-32 (CSB)

You [will] see Abraham, Isaac, and Jacob and all the prophets in the kingdom of God. Luke 13.28

Jesus said to him, "Today salvation has come to this house, because this man, too, is a son of Abraham."   Luke 19.9

> I say to you that many will come from the east and the west, and will take their places at the feast with Abraham, Isaac, and Jacob in the kingdom of heaven.   Matthew 8.11

> His help he has given to Israel, his servant, so that he might keep in mind his mercy to Abraham and his children for ever, just as he promised.   Luke 1:54-55 **(BBE)**

> To them who are good to you will I give blessing, and on him who does you wrong will I put my curse: and you will become a name of blessing to all the families of the earth.   Genesis 12:3 **(BBE)**

All the rest who are not the children of Abraham will not be in heaven and will reap sorrow on the earth.

There is a difference between Abrahams children and what we commonly call or think of as Jews (the "Judeans" mentioned in the New Testament).

Interestingly, someone can be a 'dna Jew', a physical descendant of Abraham - *but still not be*

Abraham's child <u>according to the covenant blessing</u>.

However *all* of Abrahams true children are *Jews.*

So that means some physical Jews are Abrahams children according to the covenant - and some are not.

It also means some who were not physical Jews before, are now true children of Abraham - and are true Jews according to the covenant.

How can that be – **it's because the Jewish Messiah upgraded the original covenant by birth to now be the new covenant by the second birth.**

The Bible is very clear about who is Abraham's child - and thus who is a Jew. It is simply what the Bible has said from Genesis on.

Yet today's church practices often seem blind to these facts - because the devil has been running a campaign of confusion to get between you and your blessings - it's an eclipse of the truth.

<u>This book will teach you how you can tell if you are one of Abrahams children and thus a Jew according to the covenant blessing</u>.

You will learn the blessings that belong to Abraham's children.

Introduction

Abraham was the first Jew.

Everyone agrees on that - Jews, Christians, bible scholars, historians.

The orthodox Jews of today say that someone "is Jewish" if their mother was Jewish.

But Abraham's mother was not Jewish, so he could not attend an orthodox synagogue today unless he "converted to Judaism".

The reform Jews of today say that someone "is Jewish" if their father was Jewish.

But Abraham's father was not Jewish, so he could not attend a reform synagogue today unless he "converted to Judaism".

Abraham just accepted God, he didn't have to do anything else.

By faith Abraham believed what God said.

That's what made Abraham a Jew.

As a believer, you "just accepted" God.

By faith you believed what God said about Jesus.

That's what made you a Jew.

In His Temple dialogue with the pharisees, Yeshua made it very clear -

First He says, "Your father is Abraham".

Then He says, "You think you have salvation because you have Abraham for a father - but Abraham is not your father".

He's making it very clear that someone can be <u>physically born as a descendant of Abraham</u> - *and yet still not be one of Abraham's Children.* Yeshua said "you have to be born again". Having Jewish dna is not enough - you have to be born again into the Jewish Messiah to *become* one of Abraham's children.

The reason the pharisees were not Abraham's children - is because they did not do what Abraham did -

Abraham Believed God

The pharisees did not believe God - even though He was standing right in front of them and talking to them!

So interestingly, someone can be a dna Jew - but still not be Abraham's child according to the covenant blessing.

However *all* of Abrahams true children are *Jews.*

That means some dna Jews are Abrahams children according to the covenant - and some are not.

It also means some who were not dna Jews are now true children of Abraham - and are true Jews according to the covenant.

The purpose of this book is to show how the devil has hidden this plain, obvious truth from believers - to confuse the whole issue and keep Spirit-filled children of Abraham from walking in their true blessings and power.

How can they believe God for what already belongs to them - *if they don't know that it belongs to them?*

Some of the blessings that belong to Abraham's children who do what the Lord says to do, are - Deuteronomy 28 (BBE) :

The Children of Abraham will take the land of their enemies.

The Children of Abraham will be a blessing to all the nations of the earth.

The Lord will put you high over all the nations of the earth.

You will have greater blessings than any other people.

The Lord will take away from you all disease.

A blessing will be on your coming in and on your going out.

The rest of the book explains these blessings, how they belong to each child of Abraham, and how to understand the true meaning of "Israel" as Yeshua taught it, and as Paul wrote in Romans and Galatians.

If the "church" ever awakens to the truth and reality of "chosenness" - the devil is in as much trouble as the ancient philistines were when Abraham's children showed up and God was with them.

Here's a shocker -

There will be only Jews in Heaven.

When you understand what this book is saying - and this book is just repeating what the Bible says - the only people in Heaven are those who believe in the Lord Jesus Christ.

Those who believe in Yeshua the Lord the Messiah are also Abraham's children.

All of Abraham's true children are "the Jews".

So if you are in Messiah Yeshua you are one of Abraham's children and thus are a Jew - you will be in Heaven because of your faith in Yeshua, the same way that Abraham is in Heaven. To this day God is still called the God of Abraham.

Chapter 1   In these days...

In these days of bondage in Egypt, in these days of captivity in Babylon...

You need to know your God to survive and prosper.

Only when you know who you are and take hold of your inheritance, will you see the miracles of the Bible.

But you will see them - if you read what the Bible says, and believe it - no matter what your mind tells you.

Don't you want to have favor with heathen big shots because they see and know that your God is God?

Don't you want to command devils to flee - and they go?

Don't you want to lay hands on the sick (including yourself) - and they are healed?

Then step into your true identity - that of a Jew in a pagan land.

You are part of Israel and its long tradition - you joined the wagon train at perilous times in history - just like other Jews before you who came from godless nations like Moab, Egypt, Rome.

Ask yourself this question - when God made Abraham a Jew - did his life change?

Are his descendants still blessed, thousands of years later?

Do you believe what Paul says, that you are now one of Abraham's descendants because you have accepted the Jewish Messiah?

Good, then you qualify - you are qualified for blessings, healing, prosperity, deliverance, all good things.

Grab them, run with them - never look back.

How can you tell? What does a Jew look like?

- Successful
- Happy
- Relaxed
- Healthy
- Influential
- Good relationships
- Blessed

Chapter 2   Your True Identity

The Bible was written by and about Jews with supernatural power.

So if you're not a Jew and you don't have supernatural power, you might feel a bit out of place.

Like you're watching "them" reading about "them".
While your wretched life goes on, you poor schmo.

But what if - you *were* "them"?

You just had amnesia?

That's what a lot of "churchians" have got these days - demonic amnesia.

You see, the devil wants you to forget who you are - and never find out!

Because if you find out that you are part of Israel, and that your birthright is supernatural power -

- then he's in trouble, bad trouble, like locked-in-the-pit, gates-of-hell-falling-down trouble.

Symptoms of demonic amnesia -

- you feel like "Christians" are second class citizens compared to Jews

- Jews have the money, the success, the blessing - and "Christians" should "bless" them - send money to "rub the magic Jewish lamp" ministries

- you are hesitant to talk to Jews about Jesus

- you don't know many Jews, but you want them to "like" you

- you're not surprised you don't have more blessings, because those are "for the Jews"

- you think it's marvelous what the believers in the Bible did, but you know that could never be *your* life

etc

etc

... drip, drip, drip   ...all lies from satan

Yes, every symptom on that list is a lie. *None of those statements are true in any way.*

But if you believe them, then your life will be a lie, and not the truth.

Not to mention, that lies are miserable counterfeits for the truth.

Not a good way to live, and the outcome is not good either.

Mistaken Identity

Now - after being born again -
you have to grow up again -
and learn all the things you didn't learn before.

It was a case of mistaken identity.

It's like a case of brothers switched at birth -
more like 'at second birth'.

But now the mystery has been solved.

You're on your way to the life you always wanted to have – yet maybe never thought could be real.

But it Is-real

Identity Theft

The devil has stolen the church's identity.

He wants you to believe that it's the unsaved 'jews' who have it all - the money, the smarts, the influence.

And poor little 'Churchians' are left with the crumbs.

That's not the way it's supposed to be.

You're supposed to be the head, not the tail.

The 'jews' are supposed to be jealous of *you*!

But of course they're not, who would be?

But when you come into your true Identity - they *will* become jealous - because of the blessing - and because of the Power of God shown forth in you.

That's what it's all about anyway - the Power of God.

That's made the Israelites famous - *because God showed up for them.*

If you want to be respected in the spiritual realm, that's what you have to have.

That's your **True Identity**.

Chapter 3   Claim your inheritance

Don't let it be stolen from you.

All you have to do to let it be stolen from you is - nothing.

Just do nothing and satan will sneak off with it.

Do you want to live above and not beneath?

Then you have to claim your inheritance - and fight for it!

Want to be debt free?

Then you will have to claim your inheritance - and fight each day until you receive it.

God has given these things to you - just like He gave them to your ancestors, the Israelites.

He showed them the Promised Land, full of milk and honey.

Then He told them to enter and take the land.

Then they had to fight for it.

And only two of the twelve spies had the will to

fight - the others gave up before they started - those who gave up never got out of the wilderness - they stayed there their whole lives - broke, and living far below what they could have had.

Only Joshua and Caleb - who fought - claimed their inheritance and lived in abundance with their families.

The devil will surely tell some who read this book "you're not a Jew - your granpa was Barney and your granma was Matilda - who do you think you are!"

You tell the devil –

> **"I am the Chosen of God - by the Blood of Yeshua Jesus - my foot will possess the Land everywhere I step - and neither you nor all your demons can defeat me - because I belong to Yeshua the Lord the Anointed One of Israel!!!"**

Chapter 4   There is no blessing outside Abrahams seed

Think about it, God said that all nations will be blessed through the descendants of Abraham - and especially, though not exclusively, through the descendants of Isaac and Jacob.

So if any blessing is to come from you, then you will have to believe that you are Abraham's seed and receive your inheritance.

For there is no blessing on this earth except from Abraham's children.

If you want blessing then that's where you will have to go to get it.

Do you want to be blessed?

You will have to get it from Abraham's Seed - the Lion of the Tribe of Judah - and also from Abraham's other children - saved and even unsaved sometimes.

If you want to get blessing you have to go to one of Abraham's children.

If you want to bless others you have to be one of Abraham's children.

It's pretty simple how it works.

God has set up a system to bless all Nations.

The blessing is in the holy Nation of Abraham's Children.

It is nowhere else.

There may seem to be "blessings" elsewhere but they have sorrow added with them and they are temporary things that don't lead to life.

<u>So who are Abraham's children?</u>

They are the people who have become Abraham's children by believing in Yeshua the Jewish Messiah.

Because the "natural branches" - physical descendants of Abraham - were "broken off" - taken out of the Olive Tree of Blessing - it doesn't matter anymore how you were born - who your parents were - just like it didn't matter who Abraham's parents were or what nation he was born from (it never has mattered).

So the group of people - fanning out across the earth - who have become like Abraham, trusting in the God of Israel - these are Abraham's children today.

Some of them have the physical dna of Abraham, some don't, it doesn't matter.

Now what about the physical descendants of Abraham? what of them?

Paul says they are "beloved for the father's sake".

That means that God will keep His promises to Abraham in every generation - he said Abraham's descendants would be blessed, and so they are - even if they don't yet believe in the Messiah!

That doesn't mean they will go to heaven, it doesn't mean they will be good people, or even nice.

And they may not necessarily be a blessing in every way either.

Much evil has come through some physical descendants of Abraham who served the devil instead of God.

We see this from the earliest time in Abraham's family - Esau despised his inheritance and didn't claim it - but Jacob embraced his heritage and became a father of the Messiah.

Only Abraham's children are the ones in whom the Nations will be blessed - these may be dna-related to Abraham or not - but all of them have claimed their inheritance by accepting Yeshua as their Messiah - in God's sight all of these people are Abraham's children and He calls them all the same thing - "The Israel of God" in Galatians 5.

Paul makes it clear that The Israel of God is separate from unsaved Jews who are no longer part of True Israel. But unsaved Jews can still be grafted back in by accepting the Jewish Messiah and then they can become Abraham's true children also.

Others of Abraham's dna descendants - physical Jews and Arabs - may bring blessings because they are beloved for the father's sake, but not necessarily will they be in heaven - because there is salvation only in the Name of Yeshua - there is no other name by which anyone may be saved.

⇨   This is why Yeshua said "you must be born again" - having the dna of Abraham is not enough - by being born again into Messiah is how we *become* Abraham's children.

Chapter 5   Who was the first Jew?

You will have a new awareness from this revelation.

The first Jew was Abraham, and all Jews come from him, and are his children.

When you realize that God has made you a Jew (which means "Praiser of God") just like He made Abraham a Jew - then you will expect to be blessed, because you will know that nothing can stop you from succeeding as long as you trust in God and serve Him with your whole heart.

Was Abraham's father Jewish?
No, because Abraham was the first Jew.

Was Abraham's mother Jewish?
No, because Abraham was the first Jew.

Was Sarah's father or mother Jewish?
No, she was a Jew because she was Abraham's wife.
And she became Sarah, Mother of Nations, Mother of Kings.

So if your parents weren't Jewish, you're now standing in the exact same place where Abraham was standing before God.

And you can have the exact same blessings he had.

In fact - it is your birthright!

But, like Abraham - you have to claim it!

Remember - Jacob claimed his birthright - but Esau who was Abraham's grandson - despised his birthright, so he didn't get the blessings he could have had...

Imagine what he missed out on!

Don't you miss out - it's easy to claim your birthright, just go to God and tell Him that by faith you have accepted the Jewish Messiah and that you accept and believe you are now one of Abraham's children.

Tell Him you know you will succeed because His blessing is on you - and be sure to do everything God tells you to do.

If you mess up, go to Him and say, "I messed up, I'm sorry, please forgive me, and make my mind right so I can keep going".

Jesus explained all this very well to the pharisees in John 8 (NOG) [comments added by emphasis and in brackets] -

As *Yeshua* was saying this, many people
   believed in him. *Yeshua* said to those [dna]
   Jews [Judeans] who believed in him, "If you
   live by what I say, you are truly my
   disciples. You will know the truth, and the
   truth will set you free."

They replied to *Yeshua*, "We are Abraham's
   descendants, and we've never been
   anyone's slaves. So how can you say that
   we will be set free [children of liberty]?"

Yeshua answered them, "I can guarantee this
   truth: Whoever lives a sinful life is a slave
   to sin. A slave [dna Jew] doesn't live in the
   home forever, but a [true] son [of
   Abraham] does. So if the Son sets you free,
   you will be absolutely free [children of
   liberty] [of Abraham]. I know that you're
   Abraham's [dna] descendants [seed].
   However, you want to kill me because you
   don't like what I'm saying. What I'm saying
   is what I have seen in my Father's
   presence. But you do what you've heard
   from your father."

The Jews replied to *Yeshua*, "Abraham is our
   father." *Yeshua* told them, "If you were
   Abraham's [true] children, you would do
   what Abraham did. I am a man who has
   told you the truth that I heard from God.
   But now you want to kill me. Abraham

wouldn't have done that. You're doing what your father does." The [dna] Jews said to *Yeshua*, "We're not illegitimate children. God is our only Father."

Yeshua told them, "If God were your Father, you would love me. After all, I'm here, and I came from God. I didn't come on my own. Instead, God sent me. Why don't you understand the language I use? Is it because you can't understand the words I use? You come from your [true] father, the devil, and you desire to do what your father wants you to do. The devil was a murderer from the beginning. He has never been truthful. He doesn't know what the truth is. Whenever he tells a lie, he's doing what comes naturally to him. He's a liar and the father of lies. So you don't believe me because I tell the truth. Can any of you convict me of committing a sin? If I'm telling the truth, why don't you believe me? The person who belongs to God understands what God says. You don't understand because you don't belong to God."

Your [dna] father Abraham was pleased to see that my day was coming. He saw it and was happy." The Jews said to *Yeshua*, "You're not even fifty years old. How could you have seen Abraham?" *Yeshua* told them, "I can guarantee this truth: <u>Before Abraham was ever born, I am</u>."

Notice that Yeshua (Jesus) says "you are the seed of Abraham" and "your father Abraham" - then He also says "if you were Abraham's children" - seems confusing, but He is making it very clear that you can be physically 'dna' descended from Abraham, *but still not be Abraham's true child.*

Likewise, you can be physically unrelated to Abraham, *yet be one of Abraham's true children.*

How is this possible? Because being Jewish is all about chosenness - not about birth.

And it's always been that way, from the very beginning - from Abraham himself actually. The first Jew Abraham was not one from birth - but from being born again by faith in God.

Now the fullness has come - Abraham's Seed the Messiah - rebirth in Him gives you eternal life along with every blessing there is.

"Israel" means "Prince of God" or it can also mean "straight with God" (righteous in God).

Notice how He says they are trying to kill him, but they say "who is trying to kill you?"

Minutes later yeah, they try to kill Him.

But He escapes by walking right through them.

Today those physical dna descendants of Abraham who are not Abraham's true children are still mad at Him, for no reason at all they still persecute Him.

Matt 3 John said to the Pharisees and Sadducees who came out to be immersed in water by him, "You offspring of vipers! Who has warned you to run in terror from the wrath of God to come? Produce good fruit by your acts showing your repentance. Do not think you could excuse your evil by saying, 'We have Abraham as our [dna] father.' I tell you now, God is able from these stones to raise up [true] children for Abraham." (NJCV)

Yochanan (John) is making the same point that choosing "who is a child of Abraham" is up to God - not up to men.

You can be a full blood Jew - and still be an offspring of vipers instead of an offspring of Abraham.

God knows who are His.

John even told them before he would baptize them they would have to repent - that being physically dna descended from Abraham was not enough - it wasn't enough for Esau either, because he didn't claim his birthright.

Those Jews of the covenant of the Law of Moses - unless they receive the Messiah - are under a curse now because they cannot keep the Law, and they have not accepted the Messiah's covenant.

Yet they are beloved for Abraham's sake - and because of that they experience blessings they would not otherwise have.

You should share the Messiah with them at every opportunity, otherwise they will go to hell if you don't - and you need to be fulfilling your sacred duty as a fellow Jew and tell them.

Because the natural dna branches have been broken off, they are now just like the wild branches were before they were grafted in - both are outside the covenant. The only difference is being beloved for the fathers' sake. Sort of like embers that still glow after the fire has gone out.

The blessings of Abraham's true children will always be greater than unrepentant dna children, not the other way around - Abraham's true children are what the Bible refers to as "Israel" the chosen people of God.

"Christians" who learn what it means to be Abraham's children, will experience the true blessings of the Jews - so much so that unsaved Jews will marvel, become jealous, and want to return to God.

Chapter 6 What will you have that you don't have now?

What will change as you come into your True Identity?

What if you had a high school diploma, but you didn't have a job –even though you could easily get one with that diploma?

What if every time you went for a job interview, you never mentioned that you had a diploma?

So you didn't have a job but you couldn't figure out why...

Maybe right now you don't have some of the promises of God that you want - but you don't know why.

So at the next job interview, you bring your diploma with you and show it to them - voila! you get the job!

When you pray next time, remind God that you are a child of Abraham.

He already knows this, but He says to remind Him of His Word.

So remind Him - again and again.

Remind Him that Abraham was wealthy and blessed - and that this inheritance belongs to you - and that you are claiming it!

Keep doing that every day for a week and see if you notice any difference.

Do it every day for a month and see what great things start to happen for you.

Make it a lifetime habit and watch your life change in ways you could never have imagined.

Who was the first Jew?
Abraham

Was Jesus Jewish?
Yes

Jewish started with Abraham and Jewish was completed and fulfilled in Yeshua (Jesus).

Everyone in that line between Abraham and Jesus was Jewish also.

Just so there could be no mistake, Rachav and Ruth are both mentioned as Jews in Matthew's chapter 1 genealogy.
(Neither one of them was circumcised by the way, yet it's clear that women are Jewish

without that physical sign - they showed their Jewishness by devotion to their Jewish men, by devotion to God in the Temple, and other ways).

After the Messiah came, He was rejected by the physical dna Jews who were broken off from the Olive Tree (Israel) - then New branches were grafted in and became Israel in the same way that Abraham became a Jew - by faith.

Just so there could be no mistake and so that no one could ever again keep the Jewish Law and be a Jew by dna only - the Temple was destroyed and there hasn't been any animal sacrifice for 2000 years. Thus, there is no longer any atonement for sins under the Law of Moses - so physical Jews can have no forgiveness from year to year and thus cannot be part of Israel any longer.

Now only the Gate of the Sheep is the Way into Israel.

Chapter 7 Claim your inheritance, learn who you really are

These are some of the blessings you can expect when you embrace your True Identity as one of Abraham's children:

You now join a long line of successful people.

Your success is guaranteed as long as you believe and obey God.

Everywhere your foot treads, belongs to you.

Angels will be sent to help you when you need them.

All the bad things you ever did will be forgotten, because that person has died.

You can speak what you want and you will get it.

People will want to help you even if they don't know why.

You will know things other people can't see.

You can speak and demons will flee from you.

Your bank account will increase.

Increase will come to you on every wave.

You will get unexpected good news.

You will find things you thought were lost.

People will want to be around you.

Your children will be blessed.

You will escape harm.

You will have confidence.

You will have happiness in many things.

Nothing can stop your faith.

The favor of God will be on you.

Chapter 8   More things you can expect as a child of Abraham

Blessing will happen because of you.

People will be blessed by being around you.

People will be blessed by hearing your ideas.

Random words you speak may have important significance to people even though you may not be aware that you were moving in the supernatural.

Unexpected blessings will come to people who do good things to you.

The only source of blessing on earth comes from Abraham and his children.

No other place.

That's how God has set it up.

He chose Abraham.

Abraham believed what God said was true.

The blessing on Abraham is so great that even those of his descendants who never accepted

God for themselves - are often a blessing anyway.

For example, you will frequently see unsaved Jews and Arabs who bring blessing to other people - even though they themselves will never enter Heaven.

This is a great mystery, and a great sadness - and an important reason why believers all the time need to be witnessing to Arabs and Jews.

The true children of Abraham are only those who have accepted the Jewish Messiah.

But the physical dna children of Abraham are "beloved for the fathers' sake" - in other words they will experience blessings on earth that other unbelievers will not experience - "it is God's kindness that leads us to repentance".

As a true child of Abraham, you will bring blessings to others - even sometimes when you don't know it.

Claim your inheritance to be a blessing.

Be happy that your presence on the earth makes it a better place for everybody.

Chapter 9   Inherited blessings you can claim as a child of Abraham

What are some of your inherited blessings which you can claim now that you are a child of Abraham through faith in Yeshua the Messiah?

"He did not stagger at the promises of God" - the blessings that you have are so great that sometimes it can be hard to take it all in.

First, you will live in Heaven with Yeshua forever.

If you had nothing else, this would be more than enough.

But there is much more on this earth as well.

Of course nothing on this earth can compare with Heaven, but most people agree that it's good to -

- be healthy

- have more than enough money

- enjoy good relationships

- have honor

- live a life with purpose

All those things belong to you because you are a child of Abraham.

So why don't you have them at the moment?

"The moment" is temporary - _things can change._

All those things already belong to you.

You can't "get" them because they are already yours.

You just have to do what Abraham did: Believe God. Obey God.

"Lord I believe you have given me all good blessings, and I have them right now".

Do you have difficulty paying your bills? "Lord I declare that all my bills are paid!"

If you believe that, and keep saying that, after a while the temporary will change and line up with your words of faith.

One day you'll look around and see that your bills are all paid now!

I know a man who got tired of paying interest every month on credit cards, so he started saying in faith "I don't need credit cards, I have a debit card backed by $1 million in cash!"

A couple years later, the bank mailed him a new debit card for accounts which had over $1 million cash in them!

If you believe that God flung the stars out from His fingers, then it's easy to believe that he can effortlessly pay all your bills.

I know people where some killer disease "ran in their family". But they decided "that's not going to happen to me - because I am one of Abraham's children!"

I know more than one person like that, who are now the oldest man or woman in their family line.

The power of being a child of Abraham is greater than the family curses the devil tries to put on people.

I see a great evil in this country - principalities of sickness work overtime to persuade people to talk themselves into their own graves.

Remember that "life and death are in the power of the tongue".

The devil uses scripture sometimes to kill people - did you know that?

Life for sure is in the power of *your* tongue.

When you say "I am healthy. I am strong. I feel good all the time. I never get sick." You are speaking life into yourself. Every child of Abraham has the power to do this.

But the Bible says that also "death is in the power of the tongue". Have you ever heard someone say, "Ha ha ha, I guess I'm getting old"? Sure you have, and sure enough, they will get old faster that way.

The government sends you a letter, "it's time to sign up and get your social security and medicare" which has the hidden message "you're getting old now".

I'm all for taking all the money the government will give you.

But don't take the hidden message that sometimes goes with it.

People on welfare get the money with the hidden message, "you're helpless, you can't work, you'll never succeed, here is just enough to scrape by, that's all you're worth."

Take the money, but say, "God is feeding me with ravens temporarily, but He will make me rich - just like He made my father Abraham rich!"

Ever visit a nursing home? Hear people "one-upping" each other about all the sicknesses they have? Think that might have something to do with why they're in a nursing home instead of still driving their own car?

I know people who still drive their own car into their 90's. That can be you also - but you'll have to harness the power of your tongue for life and speak life into yourself, every day.

Chapter 10   You have been born (again) into a good family

Have you ever thought you wished you had been born into a good family?

With advantages like "knowing people", understanding how "things work", etc?

Well now you have.

There is no family on earth more successful than Abraham's children.

They have excelled in every field of human endeavor -

won more nobel prizes
created more jobs
helped more people
than any other family

Now *you* are part of that.

Who are some of Abraham's dna descendants -

Albert Einstein

Nassim Taleb - stock market genius

Bob Dylan

Paul Newman

Danny Thomas and Marlo Thomas

Jonas Salk (invented polio vaccine)

Jerry Seinfeld (Arab *and* Jewish)

Henry Kissinger

Carole King

Salma Hayek

Paula Abdul

Susan Wojcicki, the CEO of YouTube

Sheryl Sandberg, the COO of Facebook

Ruth, from the bible

Lauren Bacall

Clark Gable

Dr. Oz

Vince Vaughn

And now YOU are part of this family line!

Embrace it.

Claim your inheritance.

Your heritage is to bless others -
and of course you will be blessed also.

Nothing can stop your blessing.

You have to settle this in your mind.

No matter which way you turn you will be
blessed.

But - you have to <u>claim your inheritance</u>.

You have to take your own promised land.

Just like your ancestors the Israelites did before
you.

Nothing on this earth comes without a fight,
because there is an enemy.

Victory is assured to us. But we have to fight.

I want what's mine.

I want what belongs to me.

Blessing is mine.

And I'm willing to fight for it.

Because I want to live a blessed life.

Do you?

I know when you read these words you can feel it inside you that blessing belongs to you.

Maybe you've felt that before.

Now you can understand why it's yours.

No one can take it from you.

But you still have to claim it.

Say this with your mouth -

"I am Abraham's child through faith in Jesus the Jewish Messiah -
Blessing belongs to me by the decree of the Almighty God of Israel -
I claim it
I receive it
I declare that it is mine"

If you only take 5 minutes a day and meditate

on that, then say it with your mouth - you will see things happen that will astonish you.

A lot of people never take even 5 minutes a day to claim what is already theirs.

Can you imagine having a gold encrusted treasure box on layaway, completely paid for - and never going to pick it up?

That's what it's like when people don't claim their inheritance.

Be like Jacob -

- value your inheritance

- claim it

- take it

- receive it

- use it

It's not just for yourself - all people have been blessed because of what Jacob did - because he had the faith of Abraham, the Messiah came through him, and blessed the whole world forever.

Think of your family, your friends, other people too - claim your inheritance for their sake - if you don't, many people will miss out on the blessings that God has planned that will come through you.

God has brought you into Israel for a purpose. There are others who need the blessing of the gifts God has given you.

You will find everything your heart longs for when you step into the high calling of purpose that God has chosen you for.

The blessings are wonderful, but the work that you will do for God is what will last forever.

Chapter 11   You will be out of debt

Only one group of people on earth has ever been promised that they would be debt free - the Jews.

If you have accepted Jesus the Jewish Messiah - that is now your heritage too.

Claim it.

What do you need the most?

Guess what - that is your heritage!!

The fact that you need it means _you haven't claimed it yet_.

Bills every month?

Can't find a good job?

Your boss is psycho?

All of the above?

And your wife complaining about no money too?

Hmm, sounds like someone stole your heritage... the devil.

You can take it back any time.

First it starts with you believing that being debt free is your heritage:

> "You will lend to many nations, yet borrow from none".

That is a promise to the children of Abraham who have been made righteous in the Messiah.

Did you know that when you deposit money into your bank account, you are *legally making a loan to the bank?...*

Most people don't know that - they think it is their money -

No, that's why the bank pays you interest, they are paying interest *on the loan you made to the bank.*

That's why in the next financial panic, lots of people don't realize that if the bank can't repay your loan to you - the bank can default on the loan and not pay you - that's the original meaning of the word 'bankrupt' - the bank is broke.

That's what happened of course in the 1930's.

It recently happened to a lesser extent in 2008.

And it will happen again sometime. In another book we might talk about that.

You can read that promise this way -

"You will lend to many _banks_, yet borrow from none".

Did Abraham have a car note? no

He owned all his cattle free and clear.

Did Abraham have a house note? nope

He owned so much property, including water wells, grazing land, etc - that he maintained a small army just to defend it.

He was far too wealthy to live in a gated community - he would have taken up the whole neighborhood and then some.

What did Abraham do when he needed or wanted something? just counted out the cash and paid for it.

He didn't worry if he got "miles" on his credit card.

He paid cash, and that was it.

That's your heritage - to pay cash - and have plenty left over.

Some people have so many dings on their credit report they just about have to pay cash anyway.

Here's how to get your faith up and take back your heritage -

Start saying this each day -

"I Bobby Smith will lend to many _banks_, yet borrow from none".

Do this for a week every day, even if you don't feel like it, even if you're not sure if you believe it - even if you feel like an idiot saying it (it's good if you feel like that because it means the devil is giving you that 'shame' feeling - which means the devil knows it's working and that he knows he's going to lose his hold on your heritage).

You are a speaking spirit - when you speak the promise like this - your words will activate hidden mysteries in the Spirit.

After a few days, you will notice that your mind starts thinking "maybe I can do this".

Good, keep saying it every day.

Never stop saying it.

Your words are slowly turning the rudder of your boat around to go in the right direction - you are lining up so that the wind is in your sails and propels you to your destination.

You will start to see things happen to change your circumstances.

This is because you have changed things in the spirit realm with your words - so your circumstances must bow because they are only in the natural realm.

The devil wants people to think the natural realm is "reality" - but it's not - it's all controlled by the spirit realm.

If your present 'reality' is less than blessed - it's because there is something evil in the spirit realm making it that way.

God has decreed blessing for every child of Abraham.

Like the Israelites before us - we have to fight to take the land.

We are now the Army of the One Who Is Worthy.

People who "talk their blessings" every day will
see things like this happen -

Out of nowhere they'll get a call about a
job they didn't know about

They might get a promotion because their
psycho boss got transferred

They might get an inheritance

God might give them a simple idea that
turns into a small business where they
make more money than they ever have
made before, pay off all their debts, and
become their own boss

They might see an ad where they can learn
to be a welder and the government will pay
their tuition - a year later they have plenty
of money

They may learn online how to manage
money, and get a 30% "raise" out of
"nowhere" just by not wasting the money
they have, and use that to pay off all their
debt

Someone may be doing clerical work but
they hate it because what they really like to
do is talk with people - they see that there
are a lot of sales jobs they can do - pretty

soon they're doing something they really like - and are making lots of money

Whatever it may be - your words will create your future

After all, they created your present...

Chapter 12   Under the Oaks of Mamre with God

One day God was walking on the earth near the great trees of Mamre in Hebron where Abraham lived.

Abraham ran and begged God to stay and eat with him.

There was an angel, or perhaps Jesus, with God.

Abraham served them bread, roasted veal, milk, and yogurt.
(Showing that cheeseburgers are kosher after all).

Though he tried to stop it, he knew that sodom and gomorrah would be destroyed.

Because the Presence of God brings the gift of prophecy...

If you want to know things to come...

Beg God to stay a while with you.

You will see things while in His Presence that are hidden from others.

Abraham left the town where he grew up.

And went to a place where God showed him.

Have you ever done that?

Some people need to do that to get away from -

- family (and ancestral demons)

- places (that might be demon infested)

- people (from the past who drag you down)

Some people need to do that to get to -

• where their blessing is

• where they can make money

• where God has their mate waiting for them

• where the church is that they're called to be in

• where the spiritual atmosphere is the most healthy for them

• where their purpose is

The last place Abraham left, Sarah stayed. That was the end of their marriage.

Sometimes men want to go and women want to stay where they are.

There's a balance that husband and wife have to find.

It can be different for different people.

God calls some people to the mission field.

And some He tells to preach to people in their home town (the gadarene demoniac).

Abraham made sure his son married a believer.

Make sure your children do the same.

Teach this to them from an early age.

You want your children and grandchildren to be blessed and happy.

When you are one of Abraham's children -

- **You will be effortlessly blessed**

- **Prosperity will come to you moment by moment**

When you read about Abraham, what is missing?

You don't see him rushing from one thing to the next, trying to cram everything in.

You don't see him reading self help books on the 'latest trend'.

He never joined a multi-level marketing plan.

He never worked for a company and never had a boss (except God).

He never punched a time card.

His wife never had to work.

His kids worked in the family business.

The only withholding from his paycheck was the tenth he gave to Melchizedek.

Few believers today are blessed like Abraham was.

Why?

Maybe it's simple - Abraham begged God to stay a while with him.

Appendix 1   What the Bible Says About Who is a Jew

A Discussion of what the Bible has to say about who is a Jew, a child of Abraham

Unless otherwise indicated, all Scripture quotations in this Appendix 1 are (NIV)
[comments in quotations added by emphasis and in parentheses or brackets]

The son of Jacob, the son of Isaac, the son of **Abraham**, the son of Terah, the son of Nahor
Luke 3:34

Yeshua (Jesus) is the Messiah the son of David, the **son of Abraham**

Abraham was the father of Isaac
Isaac was the father of Jacob
Jacob was the father of Judah and his brothers
Judah was the forefather of Yeshua the Lion of Yehudah (Judah)

John said to the dna Jews - "do not think you can say to yourselves, 'We have **Abraham** as our father.' I tell you that out of these stones God can raise up children for **Abraham**...." Luke 3:8

If God can raise up children for **Abraham** from stones, certainly He can raise up children for **Abraham** from the Nations -

and He has done so - you may be reading this book because you are one of them

Yeshua said "I say to you that many will come from the east and the west, and will take their places at the feast with **Abraham**, Isaac, and Jacob in the kingdom of heaven**....**" Matthew 8:11

Yeshua said "But in the account of the burning bush, even Moses showed that the dead rise. Long after **Abraham**, Isaac, and Jacob had died, In the account of the burning bush, God said to Moses, 'I am the God of **Abraham**, the God of Isaac, and the God of Jacob'. So He is the God of the Living, not the dead." Matthew 22:31

...when you see **Abraham**, Isaac, and Jacob and all the prophets in the kingdom of God Luke 13:28

Finally, the poor man died and was carried by the angels to be with **Abraham**... **Abraham** replied, 'They have Moses and the Prophets; let them listen to them**....** But **Abraham** said, 'If they won't listen to Moses and the prophets, they won't listen even though a man rises from the dead.' Luke 16:31

He has helped his servant Israel, God remembered his mercy to **Abraham** and his descendants forever, to show mercy to our ancestors and to remember his holy covenant, the oath he swore to our father **Abraham.** Luke 1:54, 1:73

Then should not this woman, <u>a daughter of</u>
Abraham, whom satan has kept bound for
eighteen long years, be set free on the Sabbath
day from what bound her? Luke 13:16

> In the same way, should not you - <u>a child</u>
> <u>of **Abraham**</u> - be set free from what binds
> you - poverty, sickness, family issues - in
> the Sabbath Year, the Year of Jubilee?

Luke 19:9 Jesus said to him, "Salvation has come
to this home today, for this man has shown himself
to be a true son of **Abraham**. For the Son of Man
came to seek and save those like him who are
lost."

> Because God remembered this lost dna son
> of **Abraham** His friend, and because of this
> man's own faith, which was shown by the
> acts produced by his faith

They answered him, 'We are **Abraham's** (dna)
descendants and have never been slaves of
anyone.' John 8
"I know that you are **Abraham's** descendants (dna
only)"
'**Abraham** is our (dna) father,' they answered.
"If you were **Abraham's** (true) children," said
Jesus, "then you would do what **Abraham** did."
"As it is, you are looking for a way to kill me, a man

who has told you the truth**...** **Abraham** did not do such things."

"You are doing the works of your (true) father (the devil)." They said to him, 'We are actual (dna) sons of **Abraham**; we have one Father, who is God....' (but they were only dna sons, not true sons with the spirit and faith of **Abraham**)

'Are you greater than our (dna) father **Abraham**?'

"Your (dna) father **Abraham** (who was also true Israel) rejoiced at the thought of seeing My day; he saw it and was glad."

"Before **Abraham** (dna and true Israel) was born, I Am!"

> God in the flesh said I Am the One who makes someone a child of **Abraham** - neither the law nor dna can do that

The God of **Abraham**, Isaac, and Jacob, the God of our (dna and true) fathers, has glorified his servant Jesus. Acts 3:13
And you are heirs of the prophets and of the covenant ...God made with your fathers. He said to **Abraham**, "Through your offspring all peoples on earth will be blessed..." Acts 3:25

> This is a promise to all true Messiah-ians, the true offspring of **Abraham**, who are the heirs of the prophets and of the covenant: In you all the Nations on earth will be blessed - believe this promise, say it with

your mouth, remind yourself of it every
week and every day, remind your spouse of
it, remind your children of it, remind God
of it

To this he replied: "Brothers and ...fathers, listen to
me! The God of glory appeared to our father
Abraham while he was still in Mesopotamia, before
he lived in Haran..." Acts 7:2

If you claim your inheritance, He will
appear to you too

So **Abraham** left the land of the Chaldeans and
settled in Haran Acts 7:4

Have you left the chaldeans yet? the party
goers? the new age people? those in the
occult? those who think abortion is ok?
those who want sex more than they want
God? those who chase money?

Have you crossed the Jordan yet into the
promised Land of Blessing God has waiting
for you?

He gave him no inheritance there... But God
promised him that he and his descendants after
him would possess the land, even though at that

time **Abraham** had no child... Acts 7:5

> Yet now, all of you reading this who have received the Jewish Messiah, are descendants of **Abraham**, you are his child - and you have the covenant promises - so claim them

God told **Abraham** that his descendants would be foreigners living in another country Acts 7:6 (GW)

> Do you ever feel like that? a foreigner living in america? out of step with the "spirits" of the times? that's a good thing

and that the people there would make them slaves and mistreat them for 400 years ...

> Have the people of this land mistreated you because of Who you believe? and how you live? Good! blessing is coming

Then he gave **Abraham** the covenant of circumcision. And **Abraham** became the father of Isaac and circumcised him eight days after his birth... Acts 7:8

> The new covenant we have is circumcision of the heart which happens after our birth -

the New Birth, our second birth

He takes us out of the things of the world which hide God from us - and brings us to a place where we can see and hear God inside, in our own heart

We are able to *believe* God - whatever we believe, we can have - there are literally no limits!

As the time drew near for God to fulfill his promise to **Abraham**, the number of our people in Egypt had greatly increased... Acts 7:17

The time has drawn near for God to fulfill His promises to us - because we are **Abraham's** children - it is the season of our Jubilee (freedom, success, and blessing)

"I Am the God of your fathers, the God of **Abraham**, Isaac, and Jacob." Moses trembled with fear and did not dare to look. ... Acts 7:32

God is the God of your father **Abraham**! Now He is *your* God! Dare to do what Moses did - talk to God, ask Him for what you want!

"Fellow children of **Abraham** and you God-fearing Nations [people from the Nations can become children of **Abraham**], it is to us that this message of salvation has been sent..." Acts 13:26

Interesting verse - he is talking to "Fellow children of **Abraham**" - dna Jews who did not yet know the Messiah and he also spoke in the same sentence to "God-fearing Nations" who he addressed as equal in the same way - those who can also become Messiah-ians, true children of **Abraham**

What then shall we say about **Abraham**, our father after the flesh...
For if **Abraham** got righteousness by works, he has reason for pride, but not before God.
Romans 4:1 (BBE)

Paul points out that **Abraham** is the forefather of dna Jews *according to the flesh* - the same distinction Yeshua made to the pharisees

Paul says that even if he had lots of good works - he still couldn't boast before God - only faith in Jesus counts

"**Abraham** believed God, and it was credited to him as righteousness, and he was called God's friend." Is this blessedness only for the circumcised [dna Jews]...or also for the uncircumcised [non-dna Jews]?   James 2:23 Romans 4:9

It was only **Abraham's** faith that counted before God - it was **Abraham's** faith that became his righteousness -
All people - dna Jew or otherwise - become righteous before God the same way

This blessedness is also for the Nations who become **Abraham's** children by faith - in other words, when you have the faith of **Abraham**, you become **Abraham's** child, and you will have the same blessings **Abraham** and his children have

Under what circumstances was it credited? Was he counted as righteous only after he was circumcised, or was it *before* he was circumcised? Clearly, God accepted **Abraham** *before* he was circumcised! Romans 4:10 (NLT)

Paul makes it clear that **Abraham's** faith was counted as the righteousness that made him the first Jew, and this occurred *before* the official sign of "Jewishness" (circumcision)

In other words - *it was faith in the Jewish God that made* **Abraham** *a Jew!   ...and nothing else*

It is the same today

And today, the descendants of the pharisees still think they have credit with God because of dna - just the same as the pharisees in Yeshua's time on earth argued with God Himself that they didn't need Him because they were descended from **Abraham** after the flesh

It didn't work then - it doesn't work now

Faith *before* circumcision made **Abraham** the first Jew - and it will make *you* his true descendant - circumcising the flesh profits nothing with regard to salvation

When you accept Yeshua the Jewish Messiah by faith you become just as Jewish as **Abraham** was, as Isaac was, as Jacob was

But, like **Abraham**, you have to believe it, and you have to claim it

Like the Israelites before you - you have to fight for it

... Circumcision was a sign that **Abraham** _already_ had faith and that God had _already_ accepted him and declared him to be righteous--even _before_ he was circumcised... Romans 4:11 (NLT)

Being "Jewish" (circumcised) was only the outward sign that **Abraham** had faith and that God had _already_ made him righteous _before_ the sign of favor appeared in his flesh.

Abraham was accepted as Jew _before_ he was circumcised <u>because he had faith</u>.

You were accepted by God because you had faith – it was _then_ that you became circumcised in your heart when you entered your Jewish inheritance by being born again.

The first original Jew, **Abraham**, became Jewish by being born again by faith into Jewishness. Then there followed a long period under the Law when Jews were physically born into the covenant - but they still had to be circumcised. The Law existed on the way to the Messiah. Once He came, Yeshua the Messiah abolished the Law as a way to be Jewish and gain salvation. Now, since the day Yeshua was resurrected and ascended into Heaven, there is _only one way_ to be saved, to be

Jewish, to have the blessings of **Abraham** - and that is by being born again into the Jewish Messiah Yeshua.

... And he is then also the father of the circumcised who <u>not only are circumcised</u> but who also follow in the footsteps of the faith that our father **Abraham** had *before* <u>he was circumcised</u>... Romans 4:12

Very important what Paul says here, **Abraham** is the father of the circumcised (dna Jews) *who also follow in the footsteps of faith in Yeshua* - but **Abraham** is not the father of those who just have dna - yet he is also the father of those who have the faith but not the dna - those who have the sign of favor from God as Jews *after* they have faith in Yeshua

Why do so few "churchians" today have the sign of Jewish favor (of real faith in Yeshua)?

Maybe because they, like unsaved dna Jews, really have not accepted the true power of God that brings salvation - when it's there, you cannot hide it

It was not through the law that **Abraham** and his offspring received the promise that he would be heir of the world, but through the righteousness that comes by **faith** Romans 4:13

The law - what some people think makes dna Jews Jewish - cannot bring the promise

Only the righteousness that comes by faith can bring the promise

So being "Jewish" by the law is a waste of time, Paul says he counted it as "drek" which is what comes out of the south end of a north bound cow

You should see it that way too

You've got to be Jewish by faith if you want the real thing

Therefore, the promise comes by faith, so that it may be by grace and may be *guaranteed* to ***all*** **Abraham's** offspring--not only to those who are of the law [dna Jews] but *also to those who have the faith of **Abraham***. He is the father of us all [who believe in Yeshua the Messiah]... Romans 4:16

Now look here - "to all **Abraham's** offspring--not only to those who are of the law *but also to those who are of **Abraham's** faith* - He is the father of us all"

Wow! Do you realize what Paul is saying? Think about it - he is describing "all of Abraham's offspring" - which includes those who are redeemed from under the law (saved dna Jews) *and also those* who have **Abraham's** faith - he is saying that "Christians" who have faith like **Abraham** are equal to dna Jews.

Paul is saying if you have faith like **Abraham** in Yeshua the Jewish Messiah, you are just as Jewish as the unsaved Jews who you think "have all the blessings".

He says that **Abraham is the father of all of us** who believe just as much as he is of unsaved dna Jews - this is in a physical sense also, because he mentions unsaved physical dna Jews and those of **Abraham's** faith as being the same - since they're not the same spiritually, he's referring also to physically.

... That is what the Scriptures mean when God told him, "I have made you the father of many nations." This happened because **Abraham** believed in the God who raises the dead to life and speaks things into being that did not exist. Romans 4:17 (NLT)

Abraham was made the father of many nations because he believed in the God who speaks things into existence that do not exist

Against all hope, **Abraham** in hope believed and so became the father of many nations, just as it had been said to him, "So shall your offspring be ... Romans 4:18

... And **Abraham's** faith did not weaken, even though, at about 100 years of age, he figured his body was as good as dead--and so was Sarah's womb... Romans 4:19 (NLT)

... **Abraham** never wavered in believing God's promise. ... but was strengthened in his faith and gave glory to God, because he was fully convinced that what He had promised He was also able to perform. Romans 4:20 (NLT)

This is why "it was credited to him as righteousness." Romans 4:22

> This is why God made him a Jew - and called him righteous - because he had the kind of faith that sees things that are not, as though they were - faith that sees things that don't exist, speaks, and calls them into existence.
>
> That's what Jews do.

If you're not doing that today and every day - you need to claim your inheritance and start speaking your future today.

Your present right now is the result of words that you spoke in the past.

<u>Your future will be what you speak today about tomorrow.</u>

... And because of **Abraham's** faith, God counted him as righteous... And when God counted him as righteous, it wasn't just for **Abraham's** benefit. Romans 4:22-23 (NLT)

It was for our benefit too

For the patriarchs **Abraham**, Isaac, and Jacob were [true] Jews full of faith, and from them is traced the ancestry of Messiah himself, Who was an Israelite as far as his human nature is concerned... Romans 9:5

You might as well get this straight right now - God is a Jew.

Pure and simple. God decided to come to earth in a Jewish body. He was circumcised on the 8th day. He kept the Law of Moses perfectly, the only human ever to do so. He was a Jew on earth. His Body was raised from the dead, ascended into Heaven, and that Jewish body now sits at the right hand of God, and IS God.

So if you don't like Jews, you're in real trouble - since the only Way you can get into Heaven is through a real live Jew.

It would all be so much easier if you just realized that believing in Jesus with the faith of **Abraham** makes you like **Abraham**, a Jew.

For not all who are descended from Israel are Israel. Not because they are his descendants are they all **Abraham's** *children*. ... [Being (dna) descendants of **Abraham** doesn't make them truly **Abraham's** *children*] ... Romans 9:6-7

Paul is just repeating here what Jesus said to the pharisees - just because someone is a dna jew by being descended from **Abraham**, does not make them truly **Abraham's** *children*.

This truth has been lost for 2,000 years. The devil doesn't want the "Church" to know this - because those who believe in Yeshua the Jewish Messiah *are Israel* - they always have been and always will be, nothing has really changed since "the old testament" (which is the 4th Covenant). We are in the 7th Covenant (what many people refer to as "the new testament").

The devil doesn't want unsaved dna jews to know this - because then they might accept the Jewish Messiah ("Christ") and become grafted back into true Israel again.

Jews getting saved has benefits for dna Jews and also for those who have become Jews by having the faith of **Abraham**.

In other words, _it is not the children by physical descent who are God's children_, but _it is the children of the promise [those who have accepted Yeshua (Jesus) as Messiah] who are regarded as_ **Abraham's** _offspring_...

Abraham _and his [true] children_ received the promise that he would be heir of the world through the righteousness that comes by **faith**…
Romans 4:13

The promise comes by faith, so that it may be by grace and may be <u>guaranteed</u> to all **Abraham's** children - not only to those who are of the law [dna Jews] but also to those who have the faith of **Abraham** [through faith in Messiah Yeshua].
Romans 4:16

*This means that **Abraham's** physical descendants are not necessarily children of God. Only the children of the promise [that is, believers in Messiah Yeshua] are considered to be **Abraham's** [true] children.* Romans 9:8

Righteousness only comes by faith in the Jewish Messiah. It does not come by physical descent. It does not come by keeping the Law of Moses.

The promise of chosenness, of salvation, is guaranteed to *all* **Abraham's** children - the children of the promise. You are one of **Abraham's** children if you believe in Yeshua the Jewish Messiah. No one else can be a child of **Abraham** of the covenant except those who believe Yeshua Is Lord.

The **Abrahamic** covenant is what defines who a Jew is. The only Way to join the **Abrahamic** covenant is by faith in Yeshua the Jewish Messiah. If you are part of that covenant, you are part of Israel and are a Jew - regardless of your physical ancestry. Remember that the same rule applied to **Abraham**, whose ancestry was Chaldean.

I ask then: Did God reject his people? By no means! I am an Israelite myself, a descendant of **Abraham**, from the tribe of Benjamin. Romans 11:1

If the part of the dough offered as firstfruits is holy, then the whole batch is holy... And if the root is holy, so are the branches. Romans 11:16

Since **Abraham** and the other patriarchs were holy, their descendants are also holy--because the entire batch is holy.

This includes now all true believers in Yeshua the Jewish Messiah.

The original branches (dna Jews) were broken off because of unbelief - because they refused the Son of God.

Yet they are still beloved for the sake of **Abraham**, not for their own sake - so they will still perish in hell if they don't accept Jesus - this means the true children of **Abraham** must witness to them (it is your solemn duty to do so).

God didn't reject his people - they rejected the One sent to them. But some, like Paul, have believed - and they are a blessing to the branches who have been grafted into the Jewish root and thus have also become true children of **Abraham.**

But some of these branches from **Abraham's** tree--some of the people of Israel--have been broken off. And you Nations, who were branches from a wild olive tree, have been grafted in. So *now you also receive the blessing God has promised **Abraham** and his children*, sharing in the rich nourishment from the root of God's special olive tree. Romans 11:17 (NLT)

... and this benefits you Nations. As far as the gospel is concerned, they are enemies... Yet they are still people he loves because he chose their ancestors **Abraham**, Isaac, and Jacob... Romans 11:28 (NLT)

> Some of the branches from **Abraham's** tree have been broken off - they are no longer part of the holy people, and they will go to hell unless you lead them to Messiah
>
> Now people from the Nations have been grafted in to the holy olive tree, and now they receive the blessing God has promised **Abraham** and his children, because of being grafted into the root of God's chosen olive tree
>
> This is the blessing the Nations have received because dna Jews rejected the Messiah - people from the Nations who

accept Yeshua the Jewish Messiah have now become children of **Abraham**!

They in turn must remember that they are now part of the root of **Abraham**, and they must witness to dna Jews who are still beloved for **Abraham's** sake - because dna Jews can be grafted back into the olive tree

If you were from the Nations and became one of God's chosen people like **Abraham** did - you owe a debt to your kinsmen after the flesh - even if they are not saved yet, even if they are enemies of God - every time you come across an unsaved dna Jew, tell them about Yeshua the Jewish Messiah anyway, regardless of their response

Are they Hebrews? So am I. Are they Israelites? So am I. Are they descendants of **Abraham**? So am I. 2 Corinthians 11:22

What Paul is saying here is, these judaizers who want to put believers back into bondage to the Law of Moses - which does no one any good since it cannot save anyone, only Yeshua can do that - these judaizers are saying to be "more Jewish" - but Paul says "if anyone is Jewish, I am - and to me, keeping Jewish rules is nothing compared to knowing the Jewish Messiah"

So also **Abraham** "believed God, and it was credited to him as righteousness." Galatians 3:6

Understand, then, that <u>those who have faith are children of **Abraham**</u>. ... The <u>real children of **Abraham**</u>, then, are those who put their faith in God. ... Galatians 3:7 (NIV) and (NLT)

> Paul makes it crystal clear that those who have faith in the God of **Abraham** through Yeshua the Jewish Messiah - those are the real children of **Abraham**

> If you have that faith, then claim your inheritance - and fight for it every day!

Scripture foresaw that God would justify the Nations by faith, and announced the gospel in advance to **Abraham**: "All nations will be blessed through you ... Galatians 3:8

> Paul notes that God announced a long time ago that the Nations would become the true children of **Abraham** too - through God's promise that all nations will be blessed through **Abraham**

So those who rely on faith are blessed along with **Abraham**, the man of faith... Galatians 3:9

He redeemed us in order that the blessing given to **Abraham** *might come to the Nations* through Christ Jesus [Yeshua the Jewish Messiah], so that by faith we might receive the promise of the Spirit. Galatians 3:14

> In fact Paul says that God redeemed us through the Jewish Messiah so that the blessing given to **Abraham** *might come to the Nations* through Messiah Yeshua (Jesus)

> In other words, *the same blessing that belongs to **Abraham** has come upon those from the Nations who believe in the Jewish Messiah*, they have become the same in God's sight as **Abraham,** the first Jew

The promises were spoken to **Abraham** and to his seed. Scripture does not say ..."and to seeds," meaning many people, but "and to your seed," meaning one person, who is Christ the Messiah. [God gave the promises to **Abraham** and his Child]. Galatians 3:16

... This is what I am trying to say: The agreement God made with **Abraham** could not be canceled 430 years later when God gave the law to Moses... Galatians 3:17 (NLT)

For if the inheritance depends on the law, then it no longer depends on the promise; but God in his

grace gave it to **Abraham** through a promise**...**
Galatians 3:18

Why, then, was the law given at all? It was added...
until the Seed [Child] to Whom [**Abraham's**]
promise was given had come. It was put into effect
through angels**...** Galatians 3:19

But God, who is One, did not use [angels] when he
gave his promise to **Abraham...** Galatians 3:20
(NLT)

If you belong to Christ the Jewish Messiah, then
*you are **Abraham's** seed*, and heirs according to
the promise. **...** And now that you belong to Christ
[the Jewish Messiah], *you are the true children of*
Abraham. You are his heirs, and God's promise to
Abraham *belongs to you*.
Galatians 3:29 (NIV) and (NLT)

> If you belong to Messiah Yeshua, then you
> are **Abraham's** child, and heir to the same
> promise that God made to **Abraham** - you
> have become the same as **Abraham** was in
> God's sight - ***this is the promise you***
> ***inherited from the Jews !!!***
>
> **Abraham** had the promise that God had
> chosen him, that he was favored by God as
> a Jew (a praiser of the One True God) - you
> also have that same promise now that you
> have accepted Yeshua (Jesus) the Jewish
> Messiah

This is your inheritance from the Jews! Claim your inheritance! Fight for it! Live in it!

Take hold of the Promise that belongs to _you_!

...it is written that **Abraham** had two sons... [and other children from concubines] Galatians 4:22

[one of] his sons... was conceived through a promise [made to **Abraham**]... Galatians 4:23

> All of **Abraham's** children are blessed, and the promised Messiah came through his son Isaac.

For surely it is not angels he helps, but **Abraham's** descendants... he helps the seed [true children] of **Abraham**... Hebrews 2:16 (NIV) and (BLB)

> What a great promise!

It says that God Himself helps the children of **Abraham** who know the Messiah!

You can claim this help for every part of your life!

If you have a problem of any kind, just pray "God of Israel, I am **Abraham's** child, I need help with (tell him what problem you have), please help me now!"

God Himself will help you.

God... made His promise to **Abraham**, ...saying, "Surely... blessing, I will bless you; and multiplying, I will multiply you. Hebrews 6:13-14 (BLB)

For this Melchizedek, king of Salem, priest of God Most High, ...met **Abraham** returning from the slaughter of the kings, and ...blessed him, is he to whom also **Abraham** gave a tenth of all [he had captured in battle], ...[this priest's name] being translated, "king of righteousness;" and then also, "king of Salem," which is, "king of peace." Hebrews 7:1-2 (BLB)

> **Abraham** was giving a tithe to the King of Righteousness (Yeshua)
>
> Yeshua was **Abraham's** seed, the promised Messiah, and Yeshua was also **Abraham's** creator

Consider how great this [priest] was, to whom even **Abraham** the patriarch gave a tenth out of the best spoils! Hebrews 7:4 (BSB)

The sons of Levi who have the position of priests may take a tenth part of the people's goods... they take it from their brothers though these are the sons of **Abraham**. Hebrews 7:5 (BBE)

This man, however, did not trace his descent from Levi, yet he collected a tenth from **Abraham** and blessed him who had the promises. Hebrews 7:6

One might even say that Levi, who collects the tenth, paid the tenth through **Abraham**...
Hebrews 7:9

For Levi was still in the loins of his father **Abraham** when Melchizedek met him Hebrews 7:10 (BSB)

You are in the Messiah Jesus

The Seed of Messiah Yeshua was in Abraham and in Isaac and in Jacob

So you were in them too because you are in Yeshua now

By faith **Abraham**, when called to go to a place he would later receive as his inheritance, obeyed and went, even though he did not know where he was going... Hebrews 11:8

Sometime God may lead you to a place you've never been before - it might be another city, a new job, a new way of thinking...

If you will just trust Him and obey His leading, things will work out fine

Faith led **Abraham** to live as a foreigner in the country that God had promised him. He lived in tents, as did Isaac and Jacob, who received the same promise from God. [They were all heirs of The Promise...] Hebrews 11:9 (GW)

For **Abraham** was confidently looking forward to the city with eternal foundations, a city designed and built by God. Hebrews 11:10 (NLT)

...Faith enabled **Abraham** to become a father, even though he was old and Sarah was past childbearing age and bore children by faith. **Abraham** trusted in God... Hebrews 11:11 (GW)

> Are you believing to have kids?
> Because you are one of **Abraham's** children, you can believe God for them, no matter what your or your wife's age is, and no matter if "the doctor says" you 'can't' have children
>
> God is greater than "the doctor"
>
> In fact, Yeshua (Jesus) is the Great Physician

And so from this one man, and he as good as dead, yet from **Abraham** came descendants as numerous as the stars in the Heavens and as countless as the sand on the seashore. Heb. 11:12

It was by faith that **Abraham** offered Isaac as a sacrifice when God was testing him... Hebrews 11:17 (NLT)

Abraham reasoned that God could even raise the dead, and so in a manner of speaking he did receive Isaac back from death... Hebrews 11:19

You foolish person, do you want evidence that faith apart from deeds [good works of obedience] is worthless? Take the case of **Abraham** our forefather... James 2:20

Abraham and his son Ishmael were both circumcised on that very day. Genesis 17:26

Abraham had taken another wife, whose name was Keturah. Genesis 25:1

Abraham was ninety-nine years old when he was circumcised. Genesis 17:24

For he remembered his holy promise given to his servant **Abraham**. Psalm 105:42

The sons of **Abraham**: Isaac and Ishmael. 1 Chronicles 1:28

The covenant he made with **Abraham**, the oath he swore to Isaac. Psalm 105:9

The covenant he made with **Abraham**, the oath he swore to Isaac. 1 Chronicles 16:16

The oath he swore to our father **Abraham.** Luke 1:73

When the LORD had finished speaking with **Abraham**, he left, and **Abraham** returned home... Genesis 18:33

Then he prayed, "LORD, God of my master **Abraham**, make me successful today, and show kindness to my master **Abraham**... Genesis 24:12

May he give you and your descendants the blessing given to **Abraham**, so that you may take possession of the land where you now reside as a foreigner, the land God gave to **Abraham**. Genesis 28:4

If you believe in Yeshua (Jesus), then you have the blessing given to **Abraham.**

This means that you may take possession of the land where you now reside.

The land, jobs, family, healing, dominion in any area - it's *yours* - so claim it - take it - *it's your inheritance.*

Abraham was now very old, and the LORD had blessed him in every way... Genesis 24:1

The Lord blessed **Abraham** in every way - this means that *if you believe* - God will bless you in every way also

It's your inheritance

Then **Abraham** returned to his servants, and they set off together for Beersheba. And **Abraham** stayed in Beersheba... Genesis 22:19

This is the account of the family line of **Abraham's** son Ishmael, whom Sarah's maid, Hagar the Egyptian, bore to **Abraham**... Genesis 25:12

This is the account of the family of Isaac, the son of **Abraham**... Genesis 25:19 (NLT)

> Here's a great way to feel how you are a spirit, who has a soul, and lives in a body – and that you will go to Heaven -
>
> Many people who read this book will find that their spirit immediately knows that this book is true.
>
> Yet their (soul) mind goes "whaa?" It sort of dimly begins to understand it.
>
> And their body – feels nothing, or maybe something like "when's lunch?"

So from this, you can know your spirit is alive and you will be in Heaven.

In the meantime, you're supposed to be renewing your mind.

Your body will be redeemed and resurrected, but the one you have now just can't be saved.

Appendix 2   Abraham's Children from Another Mother

<u>Abraham's other children besides Ishmael and Isaac</u>

According to the Hebrew Bible, <u>Zimran</u> was the first son of Abraham with Keturah, who he married after Sarah. Zimran was the first of six children and had five other brothers, Jokshan, Medan, Midian, Ishbak, and Shuah - all of whom had two half brothers as well - Ishmael and Isaac. Zimran's name means celebrate, singer, or vine dresser. He may have been the forefather of the great Arabian singers and musicians. His migration route led through today's Saudi Arabia, and historians believe that he founded the city of Jeddah in today's Saudi Arabia. It might be interesting to research the musical history of this city.

According to a Hebrew midrash, Zimran's children were Abihen, Molich, Narim - they were a maritime tribe on the western coast of Arabia - they were sailors and seafarers. Some of his descendants traveled to Persia - modern Iran, making them a part of the Persian empire and culture.
(Did they also found Ireland? if you look at the pattern of nose and ears - why do a few modern Iranians kind of have that Irish leprechaun sort

of thing?) A Greek historian called them banizomenes - meaning to dwell in the land full of rocks - some also translate the name as a mountain sheep man. They were a maritime tribe dwelling on the western coast of Arabia, and could possibly have sailed to Ireland. If you've ever been to the Emerald Isle, you know there are many hills and cliffs over the sea with sheep tended by Irish (Iranian?) shepherds.

Jokshan was the 2nd out of 6 children, the second son of Keturah with Abraham. His migration route was through today's Saudi Arabia, Yemen, and Oman. A possible translation for his name - is hardness, or a knocking (on a door), although the actual meaning is unknown.

He is noted in Flavius Josephus writings about the Jews, who called him Jazar. Josephus wrote that all of Abraham's sons including Jokshan were "men of courage and had sagacious (aka wise, discerning) minds".

His children were Sheba and Dedan (implying a possible connection to the Queen of Sheba who came to meet King Solomon).

In 2017 when six leading Arab nations banded together to fight terrorism, two of them came from Abraham's son Jokshan - Bahrain, Kuwait, Oman (Jokshan), Qatar, Saudi Arabia (Jokshan), and the United Arab Emirates.

Medan, 3rd out of 6 children, his name means conflict, contention. His likely settlement was in upper Arabia, and in a city in Indonesia named Medan, probably because he was a seafaring man. He could be also connected to the Medan people of Iran and Iraq. Very little specific information exists about who he was, his whereabouts, and his offspring.

Midian, 4th out of 6 children, from his name came the region of Midian, the place of the Midianites. One of the famous Midianites was Moses' father-in-law Jethro the priest. Midianities are mentioned in Genesis, Exodus, Numbers, Joshua, Judges, 1 Kings, 1 Chronicles, Isaiah, Habakkuk, and Acts. Their whereabouts was near the Gulf of Aqaba - near today's Saudi Arabian town of Tabuk. The tribe was nomadic. The name meant place of judgement. His offspring were Ephah, Epher, Hanoch (Enoch), Abida, and Eldaah. It is commonly believed they intermarried with the Ishmaelites.

Ishbak was the 5th out of 6 children, his name's meaning was to leave, let go. His name is sometimes also spelled as Jisbak or Josabak. His descendants may be the people known as Jasbuqu. Little else is known about him.

Shuah was the 6th out of 6 children, the

youngest of the sons of Abraham and Keturah. His whereabouts was in northern Mesopotamia - the northern region of today's Syria. The land at the time was named after him - the land of Shuakh. Job's friend Bildad was a Shuhite therefore it seems that a tribe came from him. There are various explanations for his name's meaning - including wealth, noble, prosperity, prostration, bowing low.

The mystery of Abraham's hidden children...

There is a mystery how these sons of Abraham traveled and became nations that we know even until today - but there is no question they have become great nations and wealthy, just as God promised Abraham.

The Hidden Tribes of Abraham

We know that only two tribes of Israel are known today - Judah and Benjamin - while 10 other tribes of Israel still exist but their whereabouts and descendants are unknown (Asher, Dan, Ephraim, Gad, Issachar, Manasseh, Naphtali, Reuben, Simeon, and Zebulun). We're getting clues from dna about where some of them may be, but we don't have the whole picture yet. We may provide some of the tantalizing details in another book.

Besides the famous "ten lost tribes" descended from Abraham - there are at least another "Six Hidden Tribes of Abraham" from his other sons with Keturah.... Zimran, Jokshan, Medan, Midian, Ishbak, and Shuah.

Counting Ishmael his first son with Sarah, there are at least 19 Tribes of Abraham from his 19 sons - 17 of which are now Hidden - and only two of which we have much information on.

Arabs and Jews are a lot alike - both descended from Abraham, both following religions that are not the 7th Covenant. Both are blessed in this world, both will be blessed more abundantly when they know Yeshua.

Appendix 3   Healing Promises for Abraham's Children

But for you who revere my name, the sun of righteousness will rise with healing in its wings. Malachi 4:2

God anointed Jesus of Nazareth with the Holy Spirit and power, and he went around doing good and healing all who were under the power of the devil.   Luke 9:6

So they set out and went from village to village, proclaiming the good news and healing people everywhere.   Acts 10:38

Jesus went throughout Galilee, teaching in their synagogues, proclaiming the good news of the kingdom, and healing every disease and sickness among the people.   Matthew 4:23

...to another faith by the same Spirit, to another gifts of healing by that one Spirit. 1 Corinthians 12:9

Then your light will break forth like the dawn, and your healing will quickly appear. Isaiah 58:8

The Lord will keep you free from every disease. Deuteronomy 7:15

I will protect you from illness.
Exodus 23:25 (NLT)

The LORD will sustain him on his sickbed; you will heal him on the bed where he lies.
Psalm 41:3 (CSB)

He sent Yeshua His Word made flesh and healed all their diseases, and delivered them from destruction.   Psalm 107:20 (NJCV)

He heals the brokenhearted and binds up their wounds.   Psalm 147:3

Pleasant words are a honeycomb, sweet to the soul and healing to the body.
Proverbs 16:24 (BSB)

Lord, your discipline is good, for it leads to life and health. You restore my health and allow me to live! Isaiah 38:16 (NLT)

But He was pierced for our transgressions, He was bruised for our iniquities; the punishment that brought us peace was on Him, and by His stripes we are healed.   Isaiah 53:5

Heal me, O Lord, and I shall be healed; save me, and I shall be saved, for you are my praise. Jeremiah 17:14 (KJV)

I will restore health to you, and I will heal your wounds, says the Lord. Jeremiah 30:17 (KJV)

See, I will make [you] healthy and well again, I will make [you] healed; I will let [you] see abundant peace, prosperity, and safety. Jeremiah 33:6 (BBE)

Is anyone among you sick? Let him call for the elders of the church, and let them pray over him, and anoint him with oil in the name of the Lord.   James 5:14

By the prayer of faith the sick man will be made well, he will be raised up by the Lord, and he will have forgiveness for any sin which he has done. James 5:15 (BBE)

Confess your sins to each other and pray for each other so that you may be healed. The prayer of a righteous person is powerful and effective.   James 5:16

Say prayers for one another so that you may be made well. The prayer of a good man is full of power in its working.   James 5:16 (BBE)

Jesus called his twelve disciples together and gave them authority to cast out evil spirits and to heal every kind of disease and illness. Matthew 10:1 (NLT)

Heal the sick, raise the dead, cleanse those who have leprosy, drive out demons. Freely you have received; freely give.   Matthew 10:8

Pray against illness every time.

Don't do *nothing* - even for a cold.

Don't get "used to" being sick.

Get used to getting healed all the time.

Get used to being well all the time.

Speak against sickness all the time.

Ask God to show you if there are natural causes that can be removed, or natural remedies - such as food - which will help.

There are so many toxins in the food, in the air, in the water, in the ground today.

But God has provided natural remedies for everything the devil can come up with in the natural world.

Build your faith so that you walk in divine health all the time.

Appendix 4 Recovery of Theft Promises for Abraham's Children

If a thief is caught, he must pay sevenfold, even if it costs him all the wealth of his house.
Prov 6.31

When someone tried to steal from Abraham - he sent his army out and chased them and brought everything back.

Who steals things? the devil

The thief comes only to steal, and to kill, and to destroy. John 10:10

So ask God to send angels to catch the devil, bind him, and bring back what was stolen.

If you've lost money gambling, or in the stock market, or just wasting it on things you don't need, or it was stolen from you, or you were cheated - whatever way the devil used to steal from you -

Ask God to send an army of angels and chase down the devils and bring everything back to you - keep asking God and reminding Him every day - because God likes it when you remind Him of His Word.

If you have enough faith - ask God to restore more than was stolen - God can do above and beyond all you ask or think.

Abraham said no one would say he had made Abraham rich except God Himself.

So quit playing the lottery, quit getting "stock tips" from tv or from people who know nothing, quit answering ads about get rich quick schemes.

But DO keep an eye out for ways to better your skills, openings where you can move up the job ladder, find ways to make yourself more valuable to your company - and keep praying for God to open doors of blessing and prosperity for you - ask Him all the time!

Abraham gave tithes to Melchi-tzedik - the King of Righteousness.

This was a tenth before Jacob promised a tenth to God - was it the same thing?

In another book we may look at What Is True Biblical Tithing from Israel through the Time of the Messiah.

This is the Plan that your forefather Abraham followed, that Jacob followed, that the rich young ruler followed - and that Yeshua Jesus said to follow.

It can unlock riches like you've never seen before.

Appendix 5   Is It a Delight to You?

Once you accept who you really are in the Jewish Messiah, maybe you want to celebrate Jewish holidays or customs sometimes. Is that ok? Sure, as long as it is a delight to you, that you celebrate God and enjoy Him. What's bad is if you 'do' things because you think you'll be 'in trouble' or 'less Jewish' if you don't 'do' them. That's legalism, bondage under the Law. But just having fun with Jewish stuff is fine if it delights you and you feel happy.

Here's a test where you can easily prove all this to yourself - like many Christians, do you have a special feeling for the land of Israel?

That's because when you received the Jewish Messiah, He made you like Himself, a Jew.

So naturally you will love Israel because it's the land He gave to your forefathers.

Some people will say 'yeah Christians may be spiritual Jews but not actual Jews'.

Really?

Since the Messiah came, the only way to become a Jew <u>at all</u> is to receive the Jewish Messiah.

After you do that though, you still live in a body, your body is run by your spirit, so you are physically a Jew just like Abraham was - because Abraham became a spiritual Jew first, then he was circumcised and became a physical Jew - the circumcision was a sign in his body - now baptism is a sign, communion is a sign, fasting is a sign, walking your body down to the front of a church and accepting Jesus is a sign - many people today still circumcise their children, just like Abraham - women dress modestly as a sign.

In the Messiah, circumcision is of the heart, so you're circumcised for sure, just like Abraham - since your body has a spirit living in it, your body takes on what your spirit is - your spirit is Jewish, so your body is also.

When Abraham became a Jew, the Seed of Jesus was in Abraham's body. When you accepted Jesus the Jewish Messiah, you became *in Him.* You are in Jesus, and Jesus was physically in Abraham's body - so if you aren't a Jew then who is?

The physical descendants of Abraham who are not his true children aren't Jews in the same sense - Jesus made this clear when He spoke to the pharisees (see Chapter 5). But they are still beloved for the fathers' sake and they have an advantage over other unsaved people. They are enemies for the Gospel's sake, and Revelation says they call themselves 'jews' but are the synagogue of satan - just like the pharisees before them, who were physical descendants of Abraham but were not his children because their true father was the devil. So it's a mess - but you cannot ever be anti-semitic, or turn away from your unsaved brethren, even if some of them have turned away from God.

The Second Person of the Trinity of the Jewish Godhead is physically a dna Jew Himself - He rose from the dead in a Jewish body - and ascended into Heaven in a resurrected Jewish body - where He rules and reigns forever. This is your Jewish Messiah who will welcome you into Heaven one day. He will ask you "did you visit My brethren (the Jews)?" You want to be able to say "Yes Master, I did."

Now that you know the Messiah - it is your solemn duty to tell your unsaved kinsmen about Yeshua. You can't partake of the sap of the Jewish Olive Tree and not share your blessing with the unsaved Jews who can still be grafted back in.

It took the Jews 6,000 years of history to be what God has made them today. You just got to the party. So expect a learning curve to fully embrace your inheritance from the Jews.

Today would be a good day to get started.

Epilogue

The Blessing and the Warning

Want to know what it's really like to be a Jew?

Blessing, yes. And also, the supernatural is just that - *beyond* the natural world that most people know.

> "It is a terrifying thing to fall into the hands of the living God."

Here's a first hand account of what it's like Exodus 19 (BBE) -

And Moses went up to God, and the voice of the Lord came to him from the mountain, saying, Say to the family of Jacob, and give word to the children of Israel: You have seen what I did to the Egyptians, and how I took you, as on eagles' wings, and brought you to myself. If now you will truly give ear to my voice and keep my covenant, you will be my special riches out of all the peoples: for all the earth is mine: And you will be a kingdom of priests to me, and a holy nation. These are the words which you are to say to the children of Israel.

And the Lord said to Moses, Go to the people and make them holy today and tomorrow, and let their clothing be washed. And by the third day let them be ready: for on the third day I the Lord will come down on Mount Sinai, before the eyes of all the people.

And when morning came on the third day, there were thunders and flames and a thick cloud on the mountain, and a horn sounding very loud; and all the people in the tents were shaking with fear.

And all the mountain of Sinai was smoking, for the Lord had come down on it in fire: and the smoke of it went up like the smoke of a great burning; and all the mountain was shaking. And when the sound of the horn became louder and louder, Moses' words were answered by the voice of God.

> And all the people were watching the thunderings and the flames and the sound of the horn and the mountain smoking; and when they saw it, they kept far off, shaking with fear.

Today, this feeling of awe and the fear of the Lord (which is clean), seems to be missing from many of our assemblies of the believers.

Surprisingly, the word "church" is found nowhere in the Bible, the Hebrew word used is "qahal" which means "assembly" or "multitude". The early Jews on the mountain also were an assembly before the Lord.

This assembly was about to get a message of blessing and hope. And also a warning that *once you enter in to this blessing, you cannot leave.* There is no going back.

The Covenant is forever. As long as you obey the Lord, you will live in blessing forever – forever on this earth, and forever in Heaven.

But if you don't obey, you will find out what the first Jews found out the hard way – *the blessings come only with obedience.*

There will be others besides this author who will come and teach in detail how you can stay in the Place of Blessing. That's for later. Right now, this is a small taste of who you really are in Israel, the blessings that you can rightfully claim as your own – and also a warning not to treat lightly *who you are.*

[comments in brackets]

The Blessings for Obedience

Now if you faithfully obey the voice of the LORD your God and are careful to follow all His commandments I am giving you today, the LORD your God will set you high above all the nations of the earth. All these blessings will come upon you and overtake you, if you will obey the voice of the LORD your God:

You will be blessed in the city and blessed in the country.

Your descendants will be blessed.

The produce of your land [your business] will be blessed.

The offspring of your livestock, the calves of your herds, and the lambs of your flocks, will be blessed.

Your basket and kneading bowl will be blessed.

You will be blessed when you come in.

And you will be blessed when you go out.

The LORD will cause the enemies who rise up against you to be defeated before you. They will march out against you in one direction but flee from you in seven.

The LORD will decree a blessing on your barns [bank accounts] and on everything to which you put your hand.

The LORD your God will bless you in the land [home ownership] He is giving you.

The LORD will establish you as His holy people, just as He has sworn to you, if you keep the commandments of the LORD your God and walk in His ways.

Then all the peoples of the earth will see that you are called by the Name of Yeshua the LORD, and they will stand in awe of you.

The LORD will make you prosper abundantly with children.

The LORD will prosper the offspring of your livestock, and the produce of your fields, in the land the LORD swore to your fathers to give you [you will be a property owner].

The LORD will open the heavens, His abundant storehouse, to send rain to your land in season and to bless all the work of your hands.

You will lend to many nations, but borrow from none.

The LORD will make you the head and not the tail.

You will only move upward and never downward, if you hear and carefully follow the commandments of the LORD your God, which I am giving you today.

Do not turn aside to the right or to the left from any of the words I command you today, and do not go after other gods to serve them.

It's a fact on this earth that there is good and evil. Adam and Eve found that out the hard way. They had it made, and threw it all away.

The first Jews had it made also, but many of them did not get all the blessings they could have had, because they disobeyed the Lord.

Today, sadly, many sweet believers are living to

some extent in a place of less blessing, because they may have never been taught that even though they have been set apart for blessing, if they don't follow what Yeshua taught, they may not receive those blessings. Those who have faith in Yeshua will go to Heaven. But their reward on earth, and their position in Heaven, depends on obeying the Lord. Don't take it lightly. God wants you to have *all the blessings.*

It cost Him everything to give these blessings to you, and it will cost you everything to receive them.

Yeshua said –

All who want to be my student and learn My ways, must cling to me more than to parents, wife, children, or earthly relatives - more than to all of their own wishes and desires. You can't be my student without giving up everything else for me.
To be able to learn My ways, you must hate everyone and everything else by comparison - even leave behind your own life.
Luke 14 (NJCV)

He Is your Father and He loves you. But there are some things you cannot do when you are called by the Name of the Lord.

In the Covenant of the Law there were curses for

disobedience. But we have been redeemed from the curse of the Law.

In the New Covenant that we have with Yeshua the Jewish Messiah, there are blessings for obedience.

What about disobedience? That brings an absence of blessings. The blessings just won't show up unless you are trying to obey God.

But what if you're not perfect? We have forgiveness available to us for every mistake we have made, for the mistakes we will make today, and for mistakes we haven't even made yet.

A true believer tries to do right, tries to do what God wants. If he or she messes up, they go to Yeshua and get forgiveness, then keep on going. Those are the believers who will get the blessings by faith.

As long as he or she is trying to serve God, a believer can make a lot of mistakes and still make it to Heaven.

But the more we obey God's rules, which are made for our good, the greater the rewards we will receive - because these blessings come from our covenant relationship with God.

You can't do anything to earn salvation – that is

by faith in Yeshua only.

But you can receive rewards and blessings by your obedience mixed with faith.

Salvation is free – but the more you live for God, the greater your blessings will be.

You cannot go against the Covenant and expect blessings. You have to be trying to keep the Covenant to get the blessings.

The point is, if you want to enter in to the Blessings of the Jews which belong to you, understand that this is a relationship with a Lord and King who is all powerful and wants you to be part of His Bride, the Bride of Messiah.

That explains why there were curses under the Law – who wants to marry a woman who cheats on him? Who wants a bride who jumps in bed with other guys? If a powerful man is cheated on, does he keep buying presents for his "wife" while she is in someone else's bed? I don't think so.

God is a jealous God. We all understand jealousy because we are made in His image.

So, be faithful to Him and you will live forever in His blessings. It says He will give you anything you ask for, because you belong to Him in His covenant.

But you have to take this very seriously, the same as if you were contemplating marriage – because you are.

When you get married you can't continue sleeping around, and you're actually marrying God.

It's a covenant - you can't do things against the covenant and expect to get the blessings.

Some people go against the earthly marriage covenant and then they wonder why their spouse has an attitude.

Mark 16.17 **(NLT) (KJV) (BLB)** [comments in brackets] -

These miraculous signs will accompany those who believe in Me [Yeshua the Messiah] -

In My Name they will cast out demons.

They will speak in new languages.

They will take up snakes.

If they drink poison, it will not harm them.

They will lay their hands on the sick and they

will be healed.

You will lend to many nations – and borrow from none [YOU WILL BE DEBT FREE by your faith and your obedience to the Word].

You who were from the Nations have now been made a light to all Nations. Fulfill your destiny and you will be blessed.

Made in the USA
Columbia, SC
07 July 2019